Comprehension Activity Book

for ages 8-9

This CGP book is bursting with fun activities to build up children's skills and confidence.

It's ideal for extra practice to reinforce what they're learning in primary school. Enjoy!

Published by CGP

Editors:
Andy Cashmore, Rachel Craig-McFeely and Katya Parkes

With thanks to Becca Lakin and Juliette Green for the proofreading.

With thanks to Emily Smith for the copyright research.

ISBN: 978 1 78908 713 0

Printed by W&G Baird Ltd, Antrim.
Cover and graphics used throughout the book © www.edu-clips.com
Cover design concept by emc design ltd.

Text, design, layout and original illustrations © Coordination Group Publications Ltd. (CGP) 2021
All rights reserved.

Photocopying this book is not permitted, even if you have a CLA licence.
Extra copies are available from CGP with next day delivery • 0800 1712 712 • www.cgpbooks.co.uk

Contents

A Long Climb	2
The Board Game Designer	4
Finding the Beast	6
Ways to Communicate	8
The Heroic Dog	10
Sadiq the Super Spy	12
Puzzle: The Scientists' Stories	14
The Weary Knight	16
Maddie Twigs: Rockstar	18
Kwame the Ghost	20
Rise and Shine	22
The Legend of Nian	24
Theatre Through the Ages	26
Answers	28

A Long Climb

First Read This

Take a look at this story about a mountain climbing trip.

Hayley leant against a nearby boulder. She just needed a little rest, but before she could catch her breath, Clyde marched past her.

"There's no time to stop," Clyde said. "If you'd trained for this climb like I told you to, you wouldn't be struggling."

Hayley couldn't tell what was causing her more discomfort — the pain in her knees or Clyde's constant scoldings.

"Can we set up the tent for the night here?" Hayley pleaded.

Clyde responded with an icy stare and pointed up the mountain. Perched on top of a high ridge was their destination — a luxury lodge, lit up with warm, inviting lights. An all-you-can-eat buffet, a swimming pool and a snug room awaited them.

The trek was meant to take two days, with the first night spent camping along the trail, but Clyde was determined to complete the route in one. Nothing was going to stop him.

Hayley trudged in front of Clyde. The sky was growing dark, making the narrow, uneven path even more treacherous. As she stepped up onto a rock, she heard a yelp from behind. Like a flash, she turned and saw Clyde clinging onto a ledge by his fingertips. Below him was a steep drop into darkness.

"Hold on!" Hayley cried. She pulled Clyde with all of her strength and, just as the ledge started to crumble, lifted him to safety.

Clyde sat on the ground, white as a sheet and trembling.

"Okay, let's stop for the night," he murmured.

Now Try These

1. Draw lines to show whether each sentence below is true or false.

   Hayley is tired at the start of the story.

   Hayley is finding the climb easier than Clyde.

   The lodge is a grand place to stay.

   True

   False

2. Why do you think Clyde gives Hayley an "icy stare"?

....

....

3. What does "treacherous" mean? Use a dictionary to help you. Why do you think the writer chose this word?

....

....

....

4. Which word below best describes Clyde after he is pulled to safety? Explain why.

confident ☐   terrified ☐   furious ☐   ungrateful ☐

....

....

An Extra Challenge

Clyde gave Hayley a shopping list of things they would need for their climb. Can you use the descriptions below to work out what Hayley needs to buy?

- This will help you to see when it gets dark. Get some batteries for it too, otherwise it won't work.
- If we have to stop and sleep outside, this will provide shelter. Although if we go by my schedule, we won't need it...
- It might get quite cold and wet on the trek, so you'll need something warm and waterproof to wear on your top half.

Did you reach the peak of success? Put a tick in a box.   ☹ ☐   🙂 ☐   😊 ☐

The Board Game Designer

First Read This

Here is an extract from an interview with Jodie Ball, a board game designer.

What's your first memory of playing board games, Jodie?

My family and I played games together when I was younger. Most Sundays, we'd sit around our dining room table after having a roast dinner and play a game. The game I recall most vividly was about saving penguins from a melting iceberg — it was intense! Those days with my family led me to become fascinated by board games.

Can you remember the first board game you ever designed?

I put together a very simple game when I was about eleven. I spent weeks tweaking and perfecting it, but when I finally let my family play the game, my sister won in only five minutes! At first I was devastated, but it made me even more determined to design a game that actually worked.

What's the toughest thing about designing a board game?

How long it takes to test and tweak the game can be frustrating. When you first have a new idea, it's fun to see what does or doesn't work. The problem is, testing is a long process and some stubborn games have taken years to develop. This *is* my dream job, but it's not always easy.

Do you have any advice for people who want to design board games?

Take things one step at a time. Instead of daydreaming about seeing your game in shops, start by doing lots of planning — think about the rules, the pieces you need to play the game and so on. From there, make or borrow game pieces and start playing the game yourself (it's too early to play with others yet). After that, you'll be on your way to having your game available for everyone to buy!

Now Try These

1. Complete the sentences below.

   Jodie remembers playing a board game about rescuing ....

   Jodie's .... helped her to become interested in board games.

   It took Jodie .... to finish designing her first board game.

   Jodie's sister took .... time than expected to win the game.

2. What question would you ask Jodie about the first board game she designed?

   ....

   ....

3. Do you think Jodie will continue designing board games? Why or why not?

   ....

   ....

4. In your own words, explain what Jodie suggests new board game designers should and shouldn't do.

THEY SHOULD	THEY SHOULDN'T

An Extra Challenge

The interviewer also asked Jodie for her opinion on some newly-released board games. How does she feel about each game? How can you tell?

Conquered Castles
I got the game for my birthday this year, but sadly I've only played it once. If I hadn't been so busy lately, I'd have definitely played it more.

Magic Mammoths
The game felt like it was tailored for a younger audience — my nephew enjoyed it, but I found myself yawning.

The Hidden Harbour
If you only buy one game this year, make it this one. The game changes each time you play, so it's always a unique experience — I wish I had designed it!

Did you create a winning strategy? Tick a box.

Finding the Beast

First Read This

Take a look at this poem about a group of friends who are looking for a beast.

A creature lurks in a nearby cave,
That's the news Jan and Stan gave to Dan.
"I don't fear monsters because I'm brave,"
Dan boasted, setting off with no plan.

Dan's friends followed very close behind,
Recalling rumours about the beast,
"It changes colour, has a sharp mind,"
"And it roams at night to find its feast."

Dan puffed his chest and took longer strides,
But at the cave, his confidence crumbled,
Inside, a screech, loud as a rockslide,
Made Dan shake and made the earth rumble.

"Shush you two," said Dan to Jan and Stan.
"Why don't you *shush*?!" they loudly replied.
"SHUSH right now!" said Dan to Jan and Stan.
"You need to SHUSH!" they angrily cried.

Furious growls caused the friends to sweat,
And while the trio fled in a blur,
From the cave came a group of cute pets,
With fluffy tails and the softest fur.

Now Try These

1. Circle the word that best describes Dan at the start of the poem. Use a dictionary to help you. Explain why you've chosen this word.

    starving   mighty   smug   idle

    ....

    ....

2. What does the poet mean when they say that the beast has a "sharp mind"?

    ....

3. In your own words, explain what happens when Dan arrives at the cave.

   ....

   ....

4. Why do you think the poet chose to write "shush" in different ways?

   ....

   ....

5. a) Circle the group of animals that really live in the cave.

   b) Explain how you know.

   ....

   ....

An Extra Challenge

Here are some extracts from a note that Dan has written about his adventure to the cave. How is Dan's version of events different to what is described in the poem? Why do you think Dan might have changed some of the events?

> The monster didn't scare me at all — I had a cunning strategy.

> We arrived at the monster's den and I called out to the beast to face me.

> I wasn't frightened by the monster's weak screech, but Jan and Stan begged me to be quiet.

> The monster growled so angrily that Jan and Stan ran away! I had to chase after them.

Did you discover the right answers? Put a tick in a box.

Ways to Communicate

First Read This

Look at this text about different methods of long-distance communication.

WHISTLING
To be heard over long distances, people from Greece to Mexico have developed whistled languages as an alternative to shouting. Whistling takes less effort than shouting loudly. However, whistled messages can be easily misheard because the whistled 'words' can sound similar.

DRUMS
There is a long history of using drums to send messages. In some parts of Africa, drums were used to send news from a village to people hunting deep in the forest. However, drummed messages risk being misunderstood — the drumming 'language' is made up of long phrases that can be hard to learn, so listeners may not know how to interpret the message.

SMOKE SIGNALS
While whistling and drumming use sound to send messages, smoke signals are a form of visual communication. Fires are used to create puffs of smoke, which can be seen up to 80 km away. For centuries, Native Americans used smoke signals to tell local tribes to gather or to send warning of approaching enemies.

RUNNERS
For thousands of years, running has been used to send important messages over long distances. Runners were used as messengers in the Ancient Incan Empire in South America. By using a number of relay runners, messages could travel up to 240 km in a single day. In more recent times, runners were used in World War One to send private messages between army troops.

Now Try These

1. Fill in the table with one advantage and one disadvantage of using whistling as a form of long-distance communication.

Advantage of whistling	Disadvantage of whistling

2. Why do you think smoke signals are described as "a form of visual communication"?

3. In your own words, explain the problems with using drumming to communicate.

   ....
   ....
   ....

4. a) Circle the picture that shows the type of communication you would use if you wanted to send a complex secret message to someone who lives 150 km away.

   b) Explain why you would use this form of long-distance communication instead of the others.

   ....
   ....
   ....
   ....

An Extra Challenge

Marlon and Nadira use their mobile phones to keep in touch. Have a look at what they say about their phones. Can you explain why the telephone is a better method of long-distance communication than one of the other methods on the previous page?

I love using the telephone. I can send you a message in mere seconds. We can have a back and forth conversation, even though you live on the other side of the world!

Sending long or complicated messages is simple too. Even if you don't understand something, I can easily clarify what I mean.

Did you communicate your answers well? Tick a box.

The Heroic Dog

First Read This

Take a look at this newspaper article about a brave dog, then answer the questions.

DEDICATED DOG RECEIVES MEDAL

A dog has become the first animal to receive the Mayor's medal in Fincaster. The labrador, named Cliff, received the award for his services to the town during last winter's devastating floods.

The award, which is normally given only to humans, recognises outstanding members of the Fincaster community. The Mayor felt Cliff deserved the award for his amazing bravery and dedication. In a speech to the town, the Mayor praised Cliff's "courage in dangerous circumstances".

Last winter, Cliff played a key role in rescue efforts during December's disastrous floods. Cliff joined the crew of a flood assistance boat, where his team toiled tirelessly to rescue people from the flood water and hand out essential supplies. On several occasions, Cliff was called upon to swim through the flood water in order to help people in difficulty.

Tina and Cliff (left) and Cliff with his medal (right).

Cliff started his career in water rescue as a puppy and today works as a lifeguard dog at Fincaster beach. Cliff's role involves patrolling the beach and aiding water rescues. Not only is he a beloved face on the coast, but he has also played an important role in several sea rescues.

Cliff's trainer, Tina, summed up his achievements: "Cliff may be a dog, but he really deserves this award — his hard work should be an inspiration to us all."

Animal charities are hopeful that Cliff's award will help other unsung animal heroes gain the credit they deserve for their services to Fincaster.

Now Try These

1. Give two ways that the layout of the text shows that it is a newspaper article.

   ....

   ....

2. Which two adjectives are used to describe the floods in Fincaster?

   .... and ....

3. In your own words, explain how Cliff helped during the floods and at the beach.

DURING THE FLOODS	AT THE BEACH
....	....
....	....
....	....
....	....

4. The article describes how the flood assistance team "toiled tirelessly". What does this phrase mean? Use a dictionary to help you.

....

....

5. Why do you think animal charities believe that Cliff's award might lead to other animals in Fincaster getting awards?

....

....

An Extra Challenge

Here is another article about Cliff. What do you think is the writer's main opinion? Pick out three examples from the text to back up your answer.

MAYOR'S MEDAL FOR A DOG?

The Fincaster Mayor's medal is a special award which is meant to recognise excellent members of the community. Although Cliff's achievements are impressive, I feel that giving the medal to a dog lowers its value. Cliff doesn't choose to do this job — he is made to rescue people by his trainer. It is the trainer who should be recognised. I am grateful for Cliff's service, but I think he should be rewarded with a treat, not a medal.

Do you deserve a comprehension medal? Give a box a tick.

Sadiq the Super Spy

First Read This

Here's a playscript about Sadiq, a child who's also a spy working undercover in a school.

MRS HALL: Sadiq, can you stay behind? I need a word with you.

SADIQ: Is it because of the poem I wrote about you? I thought you would find it funny.

MRS HALL: What poem? Never mind. Look Sadiq, I've had to talk to you previously about *not* participating in class, but now you've suddenly started putting your hand up, doing all your homework and even asking for more work! What are you up to?

SADIQ: (muttering under his breath) Oh no, maybe she's onto me!
(to MRS HALL) I-I-I promise I'm not up to anything! I just took your advice.

MRS HALL: Is that so? If you really are the phenomenal student you claim to be, then perhaps you'd be interested in the school's new programme. It's designed to kick your brain into gear and convert you into a well-oiled machine. We're calling it 'The Upgrade'.

SADIQ: Um... it sounds tempting but I have to go now — I've got... maths?

MRS HALL: Don't be silly, lessons have finished! You're staying right here. For too long I've had to deal with idle students. This programme will finally give me pupils who are hard-working, intelligent and obedient — and I won't let any spy stop me.
(MRS HALL stares at SADIQ threateningly.)

SADIQ: It sounds like you plan to transform us all into robots...

MRS HALL: (laughing) You took the words right out of my mouth.
(SADIQ gasps. Suddenly, the door opens and SADIQ's friend OLIVIA enters.)

OLIVIA: Sadiq, I've been looking for you everywhere! You're late for football practice.

SADIQ: Football practice? But I don't play foot— Oh yes, of course! Let's go.

Now Try These

1. Circle how Sadiq feels when he says "I-I-I promise I'm not up to anything!" How can you tell this is how Sadiq feels?

....

....

2. Can you give two features from the text that show that it is a playscript?

   ....

   ....

3. Mrs Hall describes Sadiq as a "phenomenal student". Circle the word that has a similar meaning to "phenomenal". Use a dictionary to help you.

   interesting   passionate   terrible   remarkable   inadequate

4. Why does Mrs Hall want her students to take part in "The Upgrade"?

   ....

   ....

5. Why do you think Sadiq is keen to leave at the end? Explain your answer.

   ....

   ....

   ....

An Extra Challenge

Here's some more of the play about Sadiq. How do you think each line should be performed on a stage? Explain why you think they should be performed that way.

> *(SADIQ and OLIVIA run into the corridor, panting for breath.)*
> SADIQ : Thanks Olivia — that was a sticky situation. You saved me!
> OLIVIA : *(shrugging)* When I saw you were kept behind, I knew something was up.
>   *(secretively)* What happened? Did she find out that you're a spy?
> *(There is a stomping noise in the distance. It seems to be getting closer.)*
> SADIQ : Ummm... can you hear that? It's getting louder...
> OLIVIA : It's the teachers — they're coming! RUN!

SADIQ: How did these pages go?
YOU: I'll tick a box to show you.

The Scientists' Stories

Jules was exploring a science lab, but a scientist locked the door. Read each scientist's story extract below and answer each question. Then rearrange the letters of the correct answers to reveal which scientist locked Jules in the lab.

1 "Did you let the frogs out of their tank?" asked the teacher with a frown.
I furrowed my eyebrows and pulled what I hoped was a serious expression.
"I would never dream of doing anything so naughty!" I said, trying not to laugh.

Hermann — How would you describe me?

serious — T   proud — M
mischievous — E   honest — H

2 I examined the test tube carefully. It had been two hours, and still no result — it was ridiculous! This is surely a record, I thought, sighing.

Hermina — How do you think I felt?

frustrated — H   excited — R
cheerful — I   sleepy — L

3 There were ten minutes left of the competition. I could almost taste victory, but the final test was particularly challenging: creating a bubbling, green liquid.
The previous test had involved an explosion, but that wasn't a concern this time. I stirred my mixture as it turned green. I had expected my palms to be sweating at this point, but I was calm. I surveyed the room — the others had purple liquids. Finally, my mixture began to bubble...

Hartley — Can you guess what happened to me next?

I dropped my flask and it smashed. — E
My flask suddenly exploded. — N
I won the competition. — A
I ran out of time. — B

14

4 The jar fell over and its contents poured out, covering me with a thousand microscopic specks of green powder.

Harriet

How would you describe the specks of powder I spilt?

sparkling — Y   tiny — T

poisonous — D   jagged — R

5 I added a single drop of the chemical into the flask. Suddenly, the mixture turned red and began to fizz.

Herbert

What type of word is "suddenly"?

adverb — E   adjective — A

preposition — H   verb — N

6 "Mrs Keaton! Can you help me?" I shouted, looking down at the mess of wires on my desk with irritation. Mrs Keaton surveyed the wires. "You're almost there, Harland. Just attach this wire to the bulb and that battery, and—" "Wow!" I yelled as the light turned on.

Harland

Why did I shout at the end?

I was angry. — M   I hurt myself. — I

I was amazed. — R   I was upset. — B

7 I was conducting an experiment to uncover how much of the moon was made of cheese. I felt disheartened — despite working on this peculiar project for almost a year, I had no results. I knew that one day, my investigation would be legendary, but at the moment it felt like a failure.

Heather

How would you describe my experiment?

spectacular — Y   ordinary — T

brief — D   disappointing — H

The scientist who locked the door is:

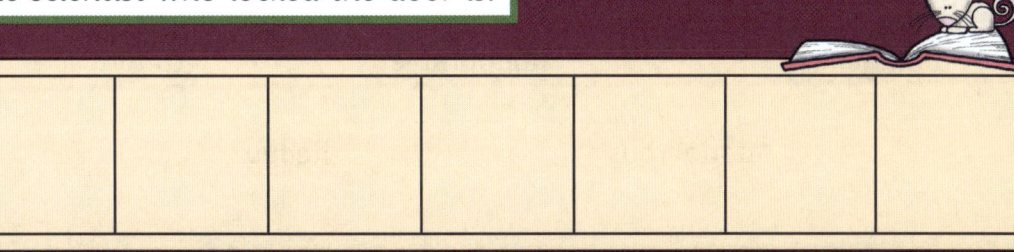

The Weary Knight

First Read This

Have a look at this poem about a knight, then answer the questions.

The night was dark as the knight got home,
The wind roared through the trees.
Then Knight Frederick, the brave and bold,
Fumbled for his keys.

Dirty from his long, strenuous quest
Fred wiped away some grime,
He searched his pockets to no avail:
Keyless, he'd have to climb.

He'd scaled the tower as a young child,
Lizard-like, climbed the wall,
But now the idea sounded absurd:
He might well slip or fall!

He shook his head and gave a low sigh,
Trembling, he grabbed a stone,
Then instantly slipped and hit his knee:
He wished he could've flown.

Yet gritting his teeth, up he scrambled,
As slowly as a snail.
Just as his last energy was spent,
He reached the window rail.

His friend saw him from across the room:
"Oh Fred! You should've knocked!
I would have let you in through the door
— Sorry, I left it locked."

Now Try These

1. The first verse of the poem uses word play. Which two words are used in word play?

   ....

2. Circle the word that has a similar meaning to "strenuous" in the line
   "Dirty from his long, strenuous quest". Use a dictionary to help you.

   magical   honourable   tough

        dangerous   heavy

3. a) Circle the animal that the poet compares Fred's climbing skills as a boy to.

   b) Why do you think the poet makes this comparison?

   ....

   ....

4. Do you think that the description of Fred as "brave and bold" is accurate? Why or why not?

   ....

   ....

5. How do you think Fred felt at the end of the poem? Explain your answer.

   ....

   ....

   ....

An Extra Challenge

Here's another poem. How is the knight in this poem different to Fred? Which knight would you rather be friends with and why?

> Her helmet shines bright in the sun,
> Her sword showcases battles won,
> "Kneel!" she shouts. "Now! Everyone!"
>
> She marches past the quaking men
> Gives orders fearlessly, and then
> Tells them all to stand up again.
>
> The soldiers respect this brave knight:
> She's lively, strong and loves to fight,
> Despite a certain lack of height.
>
> She might be stern, but she's real slick,
> Her methods really do the trick
> — just watch out for her fierce kick!

Did you conquer these pages?
Tick a box to show how you did.

Maddie Twigs: Rockstar

First Read This

Here is an extract from the autobiography of a rockstar called Maddie Twigs.

> People always ask me how I met my drummer, Ace. It's a crazy story: he was the band's saviour, our knight in shining armour — well, in a white shirt and black trousers. If it wasn't for him, we might have had to cancel the show that led to our first album. If it wasn't for him, the band wouldn't even exist anymore.
>
> It was the afternoon before our biggest show yet, a performance in front of 500 people, and we knew that a famous musician was going to be in the crowd. Annoyingly, everything was going wrong. We had arrived to the venue late, there were issues with the speakers, and then an hour before we were due on stage, the real crisis began. I remember Oni, our bass player, banging on the door of my dressing room. When I opened the door, she was so distraught I could barely make out what she was saying. Our drummer, Liam, had quit the band. Apparently the pressure of the musician in the crowd had become too much for him. I was trying my best to breathe. The same question kept racing through my mind again and again: what were we going to do? Cancelling was not an option.
>
> That's when Ace appeared. He was working at the venue as a security guard, but came over to see if he could help when he noticed I was looking blue. I joked to him that we either needed a drummer or a miracle, and I vividly recall his response: "Perhaps I can be both!" He explained that, although he worked in security, his real talent was drumming — he just hadn't found a band yet. I think I just laughed as I was so happy. I probably should've checked he wasn't lying, but I was so desperate I just believed him! And so, half an hour later, Ace was on stage with us.

Now Try These

1. Circle the word that describes how important meeting Ace was for Maddie's music career. Use a dictionary to help you. Explain why you've chosen your answer.

   irrelevant   insignificant   crucial

   ....

   ....

2. Give one feature of the text which shows that it is an autobiography.

   ....

3. What do you think happens next? Give a reason for your prediction.

   PREDICTION: ....

   ....

   EXPLANATION: ....

   ....

   ....

4. What do you think being a rockstar would be like? Explain your answer.

   ....

   ....

   ....

An Extra Challenge

Ace wrote his own account of meeting Maddie. Have a go at writing up what Maddie and Ace both remember about their first meeting. How are their accounts different?

> I was working as a security guard in a music venue when we met. I remember Maddie coming up to me in the corridor and frantically asking me whether anyone at the venue was a drummer. I don't think I'll ever forget how desperate she looked — it was heartbreaking. She could only just hold back the tears. When I volunteered my services, she screamed at the top of her lungs — I think she was relieved! She asked me to show her that I could actually play her band's songs on the drums, and once she was convinced of my ability, I found myself up on stage that evening!

How did it go? Did these pages rock? Give a box a tick.

Kwame the Ghost

First Read This

Here is the first chapter of a story about an unusual ghost.

Crash! The front door burst open. Kwame the ghost trembled all over, his colourless body flickering in and out of focus.

The floorboards creaked and dust danced in the musty air as a man and woman made their way into the hall. They looked around in awe. The house was one of those ancient buildings which seemed to have existed since the beginning of time. Its elaborate staircase twisted skywards like a plant growing towards the sun.

Hurriedly, Kwame passed through a wall, away from the intruders, and hid inside a cobweb-coated cupboard. When he was alive, Kwame had been a nervous boy, and perhaps a little reluctant to mix with other people, though he wouldn't admit it. Yet he hadn't been daunted by other humans. However, since Kwame had become a ghost, humans made him want to curl up in a ball and hide. It was something about their fleshy fingers, how loud their voices were and, worst of all, that awful feeling when one walked straight through you — it was like being plunged into ice-cold water.

Kwame shuddered. At least from his hiding place he could plan his next move undisturbed — or just wait until the humans left.

"Well, this is it!" a booming, male voice echoed in the hallway.

"It's perfect. I think it will make a great home for us!" a high-pitched, female voice squealed. Kwame gasped in horror. "What if it's haunted?" the voice continued, then very loudly she yelled "BOO!" The couple began to giggle.

However, Kwame was not laughing. What was he to do? Any old human could move into his house, but ghost laws banned Kwame from leaving. He would either have to live with these humans (not an option) or scare them away. Kwame's inability to be in the same room as the humans was going to make this tricky...

Now Try These

1. "Crash!" Why does the writer use an exclamation mark after this word?

   ....

2. "Yet he hadn't been daunted by other humans."
   What does the word "daunted" mean? Use a dictionary to help you.

   ....

3. a) What does the writer compare the feeling of being walked through to?

   ....

   b) Why do you think the writer made this comparison?

   ....

   ....

4. Draw lines to show whether each sentence about the story is true or false.

   | Kwame loved meeting new people when he was a child. |

   | Kwame's house has been empty for a long time. |

   | The humans find the idea of ghosts amusing. |

   True

   False

5. Did this extract make you want to read more of the story? Explain your answer.

   ....

   ....

   ....

An Extra Challenge

Have a look at the chapter titles below. For each one, explain why you think it should or shouldn't be used for this chapter. Which title would you choose?

- The Reluctant Haunter
- Making Friends
- A Warm Welcome
- The Uninvited Guests
- Kwame's Plan Begins
- The World's Worst Ghost

Were these pages fa-BOO-lous?
Tick a box to show how you did.

Rise and Shine

First Read This

Have a look at this poem, then answer the questions below.

It bides its time during the night,
Allowing the black silence to linger
Like the darkness behind your eyelids,
When they're scrunched up with sleep.

Gradually it peeks over the horizon,
Spreading colour over the hills
Like sheets pushed back reluctantly
As you crawl out of bed.

Its gold light expands across the sky,
Hungrily gobbling up the darkness
Like you devouring your breakfast;
Speedy spoonfuls of milky cereal.

It settles high in the fresh, blue sky,
Nestled comfortably between clouds
Like you sitting at the back of the bus,
Surrounded by school bags and friends.

The day has begun and the birds rejoice,
Chattering on the telephone wires
Like you and your friends talking,
Excited for another day of school.

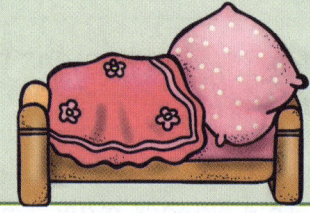

Now Try These

1. What does "it" refer to in this poem?

   ....

2. Circle the option below that best describes what kind of poem this is. Explain why you have chosen your answer.

   haiku   rhyming poem   free verse   limerick

   ....

   ....

3. What does the word "linger" mean? Use a dictionary to help you.

   ....

4. a) What part of the morning routine does the poet compare the sky filling with light to? Circle your answer.

b) What does this description show about the way that the sky becomes light? Explain your answer.

....

....

5. In your own words, explain the two main things that happen in this poem.

....

....

6. Did you enjoy this poem? Explain your answer.

....

....

....

An Extra Challenge

Here are some more poems — what are they about? How can you tell?

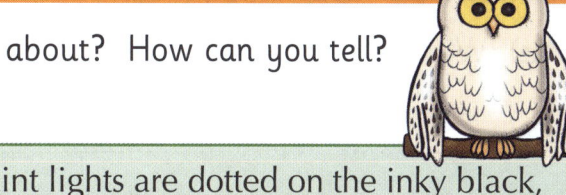

Dropping slowly beyond the horizon
The burning sphere sinks away
Like a leaf falling from a tree:
It drifts downwards and is gone.

Faint lights are dotted on the inky black,
A milky sphere hovers gently overhead.
An owl hoots softly, spreading its wings
As bats flit silently through the darkness.

How did it go? Did you shine with these answers?

The Legend of Nian

First Read This

Here is a legend that explains why Chinese New Year is celebrated.

In ancient times, a terrifying monster named Nian lived beneath the sea. The beast had pointed horns and teeth as sharp as deadly daggers. Each New Year's Eve, he emerged from the waves and destroyed a nearby village, gulping down humans and animals in his fierce, snapping jaws. The tradition had continued for years, and the villagers had learnt to shelter in the hills on that day.

One year, as the locals rushed to pack their belongings and flee into the remote hills, a grey-haired stranger arrived in the village. The stranger offered to banish the beast in exchange for a place to stay. Normally, the villagers would be interested in such an offer, but in their rush to leave, they simply laughed and ignored the old man. Soon, the stranger was alone in the deserted village — he immediately got to work.

At midnight, Nian surfaced with a thunderous roar and charged towards the village. The old man heard Nian's cry and smiled, rather than tremble with fear. Nian burst into the village, but immediately came to a halt. All around, the houses were decorated with red paper and candles glowed in every window. Nian snarled. He lunged towards the door of one house as the old man expected him to. BANG! A firework exploded from the doorway and Nian reared onto his hind legs in shock. The old man, dressed in a red robe, came out of the house, howling with laughter. Nian staggered backwards, then turned and ran from the village.

When the villagers returned, they were amazed to see their houses intact and their livestock grazing peacefully. They were so grateful that they swore to follow the stranger's advice every year so that Nian would never return.

Now Try These

1. a) What is a "dagger"? Use a dictionary to help you.

   b) Why does the writer describe Nian's teeth as "deadly daggers"?

2. What question would you ask the old man in the story?

   ....

3. How do you think the villagers feel about the old man before and after he meets Nian? How can you tell?

   BEFORE:

   ....

   ....

   ....

   AFTER:

   ....

   ....

   ....

4. Today, people celebrate Chinese New Year by decorating their homes with red decorations and setting off fireworks. Do you think the legend of Nian has led to these traditions? Explain your answer.

   ....

   ....

   ....

An Extra Challenge

Below is a short retelling of another legend — Robin Hood. How is this legend similar to the legend of Nian on the previous page? Do the two legends share any themes or features?

> A long time ago, a wicked Sheriff lived in the English city of Nottingham. The Sheriff of Nottingham was a mean and greedy man who made everyone pay him lots of money even if they couldn't afford it.
> A talented archer named Robin Hood disagreed with the Sheriff's behaviour and decided to take matters into his own hands. Along with his friends, Robin helped those in need by stealing money from the rich Sheriff and giving it to the poor. Many people were grateful for his heroics.

Were these pages a cause for celebration? Give a box a tick.

Theatre Through the Ages

First Read This

This text is all about how theatres and acting have changed throughout history.

Ancient Greek Theatre

In Ancient Greece, theatres were bowl-shaped, outdoor arenas that could seat thousands of spectators — there was one in almost every Greek city. In order to be seen by the entire audience, actors wore large masks which exaggerated their expressions. There were two main types of Greek play — tragedies, which were serious plays (often about mythical heroes) with unhappy endings, and comedies, which were more cheerful and amusing. However, not everyone liked Greek theatre, as some believed that audience members might copy the bad behaviour acted out in plays.

Theatre in Elizabethan England

During the reign of Queen Elizabeth I, theatres were mainly open-air venues. It was rare for theatres to have detailed scenery in the background, so the characters told the audience where the play was set, and viewers had to use their imagination. Another unusual feature was the lack of female actors. Instead, female characters were played by boys. Although going to the theatre was an enjoyable activity for many, some people felt that the large crowds drawn to theatres helped spread disease and made people easy targets for thieves.

Theatre Today

Nowadays, plays normally take place in indoor theatres with spectacular scenery and even special effects. Both men and women play characters in a huge variety of plays, such as comedies, tragedies and musicals (a type of play where actors sing their lines). Although lots of people enjoy watching plays, some people complain that expensive ticket prices mean that not everyone can afford to visit the theatre.

Now Try These

1. Greek actors wore masks that "exaggerated their expressions". What does the word "exaggerated" mean? Use a dictionary to help you.

   ....

2. Circle the two adjectives that best describe Ancient Greek tragedies.

   gloomy   surprising   humourless   frightening   amusing

3. What do you think is the purpose of this text?

   ....

4. In your own words, explain why some people in each era have disliked theatre.

   ....
   ....
   ....
   ....
   ....

5. In which time period would you prefer to visit the theatre? Explain your answer.

   ....
   ....
   ....

An Extra Challenge

Here are some people's experiences of the theatre in different time periods. Which time period do you think each person is from? How can you tell?

- I had an awful day — my purse was stolen as I was leaving the theatre.
- The special effects were incredible and my favourite actor played the main role — she was so amazing!
- I was sitting so far away from the stage. It was even tricky to see the actors' masks.

How did you perform in this final act? Tick a box.

Answers

Pages 2-3 — A Long Climb

1. Hayley is tired at the start of the story. — True
   Hayley is finding the climb easier than Clyde. — False
   The lodge is a grand place to stay. — True
2. Any sensible answer, e.g. He's annoyed because she wants to stop.
3. dangerous
   Any sensible answer, e.g. To show that the narrow, uneven path is tricky to walk along, and to make the reader worry that something bad could happen on the path.
4. You should have ticked: terrified
   Any sensible answer, e.g. The author says that Clyde is as "white as a sheet", which means he's scared.

An Extra Challenge

The items are: a torch, a tent, a coat.

Pages 4-5 — The Board Game Designer

1. Jodie remembers playing a board game about rescuing penguins.
   Jodie's family helped her to become interested in board games.
   It took Jodie weeks to finish designing her first board game.
   Jodie's sister took less time than expected to win the game.
2. Any sensible answer, e.g. How do you play the board game you designed?
3. Any sensible answer, e.g. Yes, because she says designing board games is her dream job.
4. THEY SHOULD: take things one step at a time, do lots of planning, make or borrow game pieces, play the game by themselves.
   THEY SHOULDN'T: daydream about their game being in a shop, play their game with other people too soon.

An Extra Challenge

Any sensible answers about Jodie's opinions, e.g.
Conquered Castles — Jodie thinks the game is good. She says she'd have definitely played it more if she hadn't been busy.
The Hidden Harbour — Jodie really likes this game. She says this is the game people should buy if they only buy one game this year.
Magic Mammoths — Jodie found the game boring. She says that she found herself yawning and thought it was too young for her.

Pages 6-7 — Finding the Beast

1. You should have circled: smug
   Any sensible answer, e.g. He says that he doesn't fear monsters, but he gets scared when he reaches the cave.
2. Any sensible answer, e.g. The beast is clever.
3. Any sensible answer, e.g. Dan loses his confidence and is scared when he hears the beast's loud screech.
4. To make it clear that the characters are getting louder each time they say it.
5. a) You should have circled: the cats
   b) The beasts from the cave are pets that have fluffy tails and soft fur.

An Extra Challenge

Dan's note says that he has a strategy but the poem says that Dan has no plan.
Dan says that he calls out to the beast, whereas in the poem he doesn't.
Dan says it was Jan and Stan telling him to be quiet, but Dan tells Jan and Stan to be quiet in the poem.
Dan says it was only Jan and Stan that ran away, but Dan, Jan and Stan all ran away in the poem.
Any sensible answer, e.g. Dan wanted to sound braver than he actually was.

Pages 8-9 — Ways to Communicate

1. Advantage: Whistling takes less effort than shouting.
   Disadvantage: It can be easy to mishear whistled messages.
2. Any sensible answer, e.g. They send messages in a way that can be seen.
3. Any sensible answer, e.g. Drummed messages are made up of long phrases that are difficult to learn and not known by everyone. This means that drummed messages are often misunderstood.
4. a) You should have circled: the runner
   b) Any sensible answer, e.g. Runners can carry complex written messages for hundreds of kilometres. Smoke signals can only be seen for up to 80 km. Whistling and drumming aren't ideal for sending complex messages, as they're often misunderstood.

An Extra Challenge

Any sensible answer, e.g. The telephone is better than whistling. Whistled messages can be misheard, whereas on the telephone, users can clarify the meaning of a message if the listener misunderstands the message. The telephone is also able to send messages around the world, which is further than whistled messages can travel.

Pages 10-11 — The Heroic Dog

1. Any two of the following: It has a headline. / The image has a caption. / The writing is laid out in columns.
2. devastating, disastrous
3. DURING THE FLOODS: Cliff helped the crew of a flood assistance boat rescue people by swimming through the flood water.
   AT THE BEACH: Cliff is a lifeguard dog who patrols the beach and helps rescue people from the sea.
4. worked hard without stopping for a rest

Answers

5. Any sensible answer, e.g. Cliff was the first animal to get the Mayor's medal, which shows that animals in Fincaster can get awards for their services.

   An Extra Challenge

   Any sensible answer, e.g. The writer's main opinion is that Cliff shouldn't have been given a medal.
   - The writer thinks the medal's value is decreased by giving it to a dog.
   - The writer says the trainer should get the medal, not Cliff, because Cliff doesn't choose to do his job.
   - The writer thinks Cliff should be given a treat rather than a medal.

Pages 12-13 — Sadiq the Super Spy

1. You should have circled: the nervous face
   Sadiq stammers when he speaks which suggests he is nervous.
2. Character names on the left of the page and stage directions
3. You should have circled: remarkable
4. Any sensible answer, e.g. She's tired of having lazy students and 'The Upgrade' will make them more obedient and hard-working.
5. Any sensible answer, e.g. He realises Mrs Hall knows he is a spy and also wants to turn him into a robot.

   An Extra Challenge

   Any sensible answer for each line, e.g.
   I would breathe heavily when I say Sadiq's first line because the stage direction says he is panting for breath. I would say "You saved me!" enthusiastically because it is an exclamation.

Pages 14-15 — The Scientists' Stories

1. mischievous — E
2. frustrated — H
3. I won the competition. — A
4. tiny — T
5. adverb — E
6. I was amazed. — R
7. disappointing — H

   The scientist who locked the door is: HEATHER

Pages 16-17 — The Weary Knight

1. night, knight
2. You should have circled: tough
3. a) You should have circled: the lizard
   b) Any sensible answer, e.g. To show that Fred climbed up the tower skilfully and easily, like a lizard would be able to.
4. Any sensible answer, e.g. No, he is not brave and bold because he is scared to climb up the wall.

5. Any sensible answer, e.g. I think Fred felt frustrated because he could have just knocked on the door rather than climb the tower.

   An Extra Challenge

   Fred isn't very brave, whereas the knight in the second poem is fearless. Fred seems foolish because he forgets his keys and doesn't think to knock, whereas the knight in the second poem knows what she's doing. Fred is covered in dirt, whereas the knight in the second poem has shiny armour. Fred is tired, whereas the knight in the second poem is full of energy.

   Any sensible answer, e.g. I would rather be friends with Fred because the knight in the second poem seems too serious.

Pages 18-19 — Maddie Twigs: Rockstar

1. You should have circled: crucial
   Any sensible answer, e.g. Maddie thinks that the band wouldn't have existed if she hadn't met Ace.
2. Any sensible answer, e.g. It is written in the first person.
3. Any sensible answer, e.g.
   PREDICTION: The show went well and the famous musician helped the band make their first album.
   EXPLANATION: Maddie says that there was a famous musician in the crowd and that the show led to their first album.
4. Any sensible answer, e.g. It would be fun, because you get to play music on stage, but it would also be stressful when things go wrong.

   An Extra Challenge

   MADDIE: Maddie remembers being worried after her drummer quit, and Ace coming over to her to see what was wrong. She joked about needing a new drummer, and was so thrilled when she learnt that Ace could play the drums that she didn't even listen to him play.
   ACE: Ace remembers Maddie being very upset and asking him if he knew any drummers. When Ace said he could play the drums, she screamed with joy and tested his abilities before he went on stage.

   Any sensible differences between their two accounts, e.g. Maddie says that she joked to Ace about the situation, whereas Ace says she was frantic.

Pages 20-21 — Kwame the Ghost

1. To show that the sound was loud.
2. frightened
3. a) Being plunged into ice-cold water.
   b) Any sensible answer, e.g. To show how uncomfortable and shocking the feeling is.
4. Kwame loved meeting new people when he was a child. — False
   Kwame's house has been empty for a long time. — True
   The humans find the idea of ghosts amusing. — True

Answers

5. Any sensible answer, e.g. Yes, because I want to find out how Kwame tries to drive out the humans.

An Extra Challenge

Suitable titles:
The Reluctant Haunter, The Uninvited Guests, The World's Worst Ghost
Unsuitable titles:
Making Friends, A Warm Welcome, Kwame's Plan Begins

Any sensible reason for each title, e.g. 'The Reluctant Haunter' is suitable because it shows that Kwame is scared of humans and doesn't want to haunt them.

Any sensible choice of title, e.g. I would choose the title 'The Uninvited Guests'.

Pages 22-23 — Rise and Shine

1. the Sun
2. You should have circled: free verse
   Any sensible reason, e.g. The poem doesn't rhyme or have a regular rhythm.
3. Any sensible answer, e.g. remain
4. a) You should have circled: the boy eating breakfast.
   b) Any sensible answer, e.g. It shows that the sky becomes light quickly because the person eats their breakfast quickly.
5. Any sensible answer, e.g. The sun rises and someone gets out of bed to go to school.
6. Any sensible answer, e.g. Yes, because it has lots of interesting similes and descriptions.

An Extra Challenge

Any sensible answer, e.g.

The first poem is about the sunset. The "burning sphere" refers to the Sun. The poem describes how the Sun comes down from the sky like a leaf falling off a tree.

The second poem is about the night time. The "faint lights" in the "inky black" refer to the stars in the night sky and the "milky sphere" refers to the moon. Most owls and bats only fly around during the night.

Pages 24-25 — The Legend of Nian

1. a) A short knife that is used as a weapon.
   b) Any sensible answer, e.g. To show that the teeth are sharp and dangerous like weapons.

2. Any sensible answer, e.g. Why did you decide to help the villagers?
3. Any sensible answer, e.g.
   BEFORE: They thought he was foolish — they laughed at him and ignored him.
   AFTER: They feel very happy and thankful — they were grateful and followed his advice in the future.
4. Any sensible answer, e.g. Yes. In the legend of Nian, the old man decorates the village with red paper and uses a firework on New Year's Eve, which is similar to what people do today.

An Extra Challenge

Any sensible answer, e.g. Both of the legends are about a hero fighting an evil character. In the legend of Nian, the old man fights the man-eating monster Nian, and in the legend of Robin Hood, Robin steals money from the wicked Sheriff of Nottingham. Both stories are also set a long time ago. They also feature a hero helping people in need, who are grateful to the hero at the end.

Pages 26-27 — Theatre Through the Ages

1. made to look bigger or more obvious
2. You should have circled: gloomy, humourless
3. To inform / to give information
4. Any sensible answer, e.g. Some Ancient Greeks worried that the theatre would make people behave badly. Some Elizabethans thought that the theatre led to disease and crime. Today, some people complain that the theatre is too expensive.
5. Any sensible answer, e.g. Ancient Greece because it would be interesting to see the actors' masks. It would be very different to how theatre is today.

An Extra Challenge

The first person is from Elizabethan England because theatre audiences were seen as easy targets for thieves in that era.

The second person is from the present day because theatre now uses special effects and female actors.

The third person is from Ancient Greece because in that period of theatre, the arenas were very large and actors wore large masks.